Nature's Children

WOLVES

Judy Ross

 Grolier

FACTS IN BRIEF

Classification of the wolf
    Class: *Mammalia* (mammals)
    Order: *Carnivora* (meat-eaters)
    Family: *Canidae* (dog family)
    Genus: *Canis*
    Species: *Canis lupus*

World distribution. Europe, Asia and North America.

Habitat. Various.

Distinctive physical characteristics. Appear very much like German shepherd dogs except for their longer legs, narrower chests, larger feet and rounded ears; wolves of different regions will tend to differ in color.

Habits. Usually live in small strictly organized packs of related animals; packs mark and defend a territory; the wolves of some areas migrate seasonally.

Diet. Herd animals, birds and small mammals.

Published originally as
"Getting to Know . . . Nature's Children."

This series is approved and recommended by the Federation of Ontario Naturalists.

Canadian Cataloguing in Publication Data

Ross, Judy, 1942–
   Wolves

(Nature's children)
Includes index.
ISBN 0-7172-1941-0 (bound) — ISBN 0-7172-2759-6 (pbk.)

1. Wolves—Juvenile literature.
I. Title.   II. Series.

QL737.C22R67   1985   j599.74'442   C85-098744-X

Paperback:
Cover design: Tania Craan
Cover photo: Scott Leslie/
             First Light

Casebound:
Cover Photo: Stephen J.
            Krasemann/
            Valan Photos

Contents

When you think of a wolf, what comes into your mind? The nasty wolf who dressed up like a grandma to fool Little Red Riding Hood? The big bad wolf who frightened the Three Little Pigs and blew their house down?

In many fairy tales and cartoons wolves are sly and sneaky or just plain mean. No wonder people fear and dislike them.

You might be surprised to learn that, like most wild animals, wolves are probably more frightened of us than we are of them. In addition, wolves are beautiful, intelligent animals who are loyal to each other, live together in families and take special care of their young.

Roly-Poly Pup

With its soft, fuzzy coat and baby-blue eyes a wolf pup looks a lot like a pet puppy dog.

And, like a puppy dog, a wolf pup loves to play with its brothers and sisters.

As the pups tumble over each other, an adult wolf stands guard nearby. If this "babysitter" senses danger, it will quickly send the pups scurrying into the safety of their den.

Play teaches the wolf pup many things. Perhaps the most important lesson is its place in their family, or "pack." When a pup begins to lose in a play fight, it rolls over on its back, ending the fight. The stronger pup is almost always the winner. It stands with its tail in the air, as if to say, "I am the ruler here!" This is the law of the pack—the weaker always obeys the stronger.

Before this pup's first birthday it will be almost as large as its parents.

Dog Cousins

Wolves are related to coyotes, foxes, jackals, dingos and to our pet dogs.

Fox

People often get the wolf and its cousin, the coyote, mixed up because they look so much alike. But if you could put a wolf and a coyote side by side, you would see that wolves are larger and stockier than coyotes.

This is a Timber Wolf—the most common kind of wolf. It is the largest wild member of the dog family.

Coyote

Wolf

Timber Wolf.

Where They Live

Wolves used to live all over North America, but today their range is much smaller. They live mostly in the wilderness parts of Canada and in Alaska. Some wolves prefer to live in forested areas, while others live farther north in the tundra where there are no trees. The forest-dwellers are usually gray to black in color; the tundra-dwellers are generally lighter in color.

Our North American wolves have relatives in Asia, Italy, Scandinavia and parts of Eastern Europe.

The Wolf Up Close

You have heard of the Big Bad Wolf, but how big are wolves in real life? Some large males weigh over 45 kilograms (100 pounds) and are two metres (6 feet) from nose to tail tip. But most males are about the size of a German Shepherd and the females are considerably smaller.

Although some wolves look a lot like German Shepherds, they have longer legs and bigger feet than these dog relatives. And their bodies look more streamlined because their chests are narrower.

Wolves come in a wide range of colors. Some are black, others are white and still others are any color in between. Sometimes wolf pups in the same litter will even have different colors of coats.

Wolf tracks.

On the Move

Like dogs, wolves run on their toes. This lets them take longer strides. For a short distance they can run about 45 kilometres (24 miles) an hour. Although that is pretty fast, most of the animals wolves hunt for food are even faster and those that are not can often escape by zigzagging and turning suddenly. But wolves have one advantage. They are almost tireless and can run for hours.

Most wolves are also amazingly strong and agile. A full-grown wolf can leap as high as a one-storey building.

Long distance runner!

A Big Family

You will not often see a wolf on its own. Wolves like company and live in family groups called packs. The members of the pack are usually the mother and father and their young, along with aunts, uncles and cousins. Most wolf packs have seven or eight members, but some have as many as 14.

The pack always has a leader—the strongest male in the group. Every other pack member knows its place and quickly learns to "follow the leader."

Wolf families are affectionate and co-operative. They play and hunt together. They protect each other too. If one wolf gets into trouble, the others will try to help it.

Leader of the Pack

It is easy to tell which wolf is the pack leader. He is usually the biggest. He stands proud and tall with his tail and head held high. He is the king and he knows it. When he approaches another wolf in his pack, it will cower and skulk, hang its head down and put its tail between its legs. Then it will roll over on its back as if to say, "I give up—you are too strong for me!" This is why wolves seldom fight among themselves. The weaker ones almost always give in before a real fight begins.

Occasionally a wolf does live alone. No one knows for sure why this happens, but it is a hard life without the safety of the pack. Lone wolves often die.

The pack leader often displays his authority by staring at his fellow pack members. The submissive wolves will usually turn away.

Always Alert

Although wolves lie about relaxing in the sun, they are always alert, looking for their next meal or watching for danger.

Luckily wolves have super senses to help them. Like a dog, a wolf has good hearing and can hear high-pitched sounds that people cannot hear. If another pack of wolves is howling many miles away a wolf will hear every howl and know where they are coming from. To do this, it swivels its ears around until it has found the source of the sound.

The wolf also has an acute sense of smell to help it sniff out prey and good eyesight to catch any nearby movement that may signal danger or food.

The wolf has very keen hearing and can detect sounds up to 10 kilometres (6 miles) away.

Wolf Talk

When you talk to your friends you say words out loud. But wolves can "talk" to each other without making a sound. When a wolf's ears point straight up and its teeth are bared, it is warning others to "watch out!" When the pupils of its eyes become narrow slits and its ears are flattened against its head, it is saying, "What's going on here?"

The wolf uses its tail to send messages too. A tail held high tells other wolves, "I'm in charge here." When a wolf tucks its tail between its legs, it is saying, "I'm not going to argue!"

It is easy to tell when a wolf is happy. Like a dog, it tilts its head and wiggles its body from side to side.

All members of the wolf pack recognize these different messages. But when they want to have a long-distance conversation with another pack there is nothing like a good howl for keeping in touch.

"I'm in charge."

"You're the boss."

Opposite page:

Wolves usually spend hot summer afternoons resting.

A Howling Good Time

Wolves seem to really enjoy howling. Sometimes they howl to gather their pack together before a hunt or to let another wolf pack know they are nearby. But at other times they gather close to each other, wag their tails and seem to howl just for the fun of it.

Some people say that once you have heard a wolf howling you will never forget the sound. The range of a wolf's voice is similar to ours. When several howl together, they sound like an eerie choir.

Some people have learned to imitate a wolf's howl and sometimes wolves will answer back. Perhaps they cannot tell the difference!

Besides howling, wolves make other sounds too. They bark, yelp, whine and snarl—just like a dog.

Wolves do most of their howling at night, but they may well decide to call during the day too.

No Trespassing!

Home for the wolf pack may be a huge area, anywhere from 160 to 400 square kilometres (100-250 square miles). The pack will hunt in this territory and defend it against any wolves from other packs. Occasionally, however, packs do join together for winter hunting.

The wolf pack follows the same hunting routes over and over again, trotting along logging roads or the bank of a river, constantly on the lookout for their next meal.

Some days the pack may travel as many as 95 kilometres (60 miles) without finding anything to eat. All along the route they mark the territory by spraying urine on the trees and shrubs. These scent markings are a sign to other wolves that, "This territory is taken—so keep out!"

Team Hunters

Wolves are carnivores, which means that they eat mainly meat. They often hunt alone to catch the small animals and birds that make up much of their diet. But usually the members of the pack will join together to hunt a large animal, such as a caribou, elk or moose.

When this happens, the wolves work together as a team. Sometimes the wolves trick their prey. They divide into two groups and set up an ambush. One group will drive the prey animal toward the rest of the pack which is lying in wait. But even though wolves are clever hunters, most of their prey escape and sometimes the pack goes for days without food.

In the Arctic the Timber Wolf's coat is often pure white.

Hungry as a Wolf

Can you imagine eating a big turkey all by yourself? A full-grown wolf can eat as much as nine kilograms (20 pounds) of meat at one time. That is about the amount of meat on a really big turkey.

Good manners are important when a pack has made a large kill. The leader of the pack always eats first and chooses the best pieces of meat. Next the other members of the pack eat one after the other. Anyone who tries to butt in is met with snarls and barks. The message is clear: "Wait your turn."

Sometimes food that is not eaten is buried or hidden in a hollow log so that the wolves can return for it later. If there are no leftovers and hunting is bad, a wolf can live for several weeks without food. Sometimes the weakest members of the pack get nothing to eat for even longer than that.

Like all of us, a wolf enjoys a cool drink.

Cold Weather Survivors

If a wolf lives where winters are long and cold, it will grow a thick two-layered coat to keep it warm. Long, coarse guard hairs shed rain and snow, while the thick, short underfur traps body-warmed air next to the wolf's skin.

The treads on your snowboots keep you from slipping on icy roads in winter. The wolf has similar treads on its feet—strong tufts of hair that grow between the cushiony foot pads. These help grip the ice when the wolf is traveling across frozen lakes.

Since the wolf is so well equipped to run on ice, a deep snowfall with an icy crust on top makes hunting big game easier for it. The wolf is light enough to run on top of the snow without breaking through the crust, but the larger animal it is chasing sinks through into the deep snow and then cannot escape.

Well dressed for winter.

Loyal Mates and Good Parents

Toward the end of winter the male and female wolf mate. In a pack it is usually only the strongest pair who become parents. If all of the wolves mated, the pack would become too big.

Naturalists believe that wolves pair for life. Both mother and father look after the young and are very good, caring parents. If the mother dies, the father will try to take care of the pups on his own. If he cannot, another adult in the pack will adopt the babies and care for them as if they were its own.

A Cozy Den

Before the pups are born, the mother wolf searches for a birth den. She looks for an underground den, perhaps one that has already been used by a fox or badger. If she cannot find a ready-made den, she will dig one of her own, usually in the side of a sandy hill.

Digging the den is hard work for the mother wolf. First she digs a tunnel that is as long as a car. This tunnel slopes up so that rain will not run into it and it is narrow so that bigger animals cannot crawl into it. At the end of the tunnel, she hollows out a room just big enough for her and her litter.

Once she has her den ready, the mother wolf can relax and rest while awaiting the arrival of her pups.

Spring Pups

The wolf pups are born in the spring. Sometimes there are as many as fourteen of them in the litter, but usually only six or seven.

The newborn pups are very tiny at birth. They weigh about as much as a loaf of bread. They have fine woolly hair that is a sooty blue-gray color and their eyes are shut. They are helpless, so the mother wolf keeps them well hidden in the den. She protects them and lets them snuggle in her warm fur and drink her milk.

For the first two weeks even the father stays away so that the mother wolf and her babies are left undisturbed. Then he begins to visit, usually bringing food for the mother. He is greeted by the excited pups who now stagger about on wobbly legs with their eyes open.

By this time they are growing thicker fur coats.

Wolf families are very affectionate.

Happy Relatives

The birth of the pups is a big event for the pack. For several weeks the pups' aunts and uncles gather around the entrance to the den. When the month-old pups make their first appearance outdoors, the whole pack takes turns playing with them. It is as if they are celebrating the pups' arrival.

You might not even guess that the pups are brothers and sisters because they all look so different. Some pups are pure black, others are speckled beige and still others are somewhere in between. Wolves seem to love babies. They are affectionate and caring with the new pups. They guard them carefully from predators such as eagles or wolverines and keep them from accidentally running into porcupines. When the mother goes off to hunt, an aunt or uncle stays behind to "pupsit."

After three months, wolf pups no longer sleep in their den.

Many Mouths to Feed

As the pups get bigger the birth den becomes cramped and stuffy. So the mother moves her new family to a bigger den. On moving day she carries one pup at a time in her mouth, gently gripping them by the loose skin on their necks.

By age two months, the pups are ready to eat meat. All the family members help to feed them. They bring back meat from the kill in their stomachs. When the pups lick the adult's jaws, the adults bring the food back into their mouths. They then give this half-digested food to the pups.

This may not sound very appealing to you, but it makes a lot of sense for the wolf. If it had to carry fresh meat back to the den a trail would be left leading right to the helpless pups. By carrying the food home in its stomach the wolf keeps the location of the den a secret from other predators. Also, it is much easier for wolves to carry food in their stomachs for long distances.

Opposite page:

Like many young animals, wolf pups are very curious.

42

Living and Learning

There is much for a wolf pup to learn before it can become an active member of the pack.

The most important lesson is learning its place in the pack. By playfighting and wrestling the pups learn who is strongest and therefore who is dominant.

The next important lesson is how to hunt. The pups pounce on twigs and leaves—and sometimes on each other! These playful games teach them how to stalk prey and set up ambushes.

This pup still has lots to learn!

Joining the Hunt

By the fall the pups look like smaller versions of their parents. They are getting better at hunting games. They practice chasing and catching small animals like mice and frogs.

They have also learned to obey their elders. If they forget their manners they get a gentle smack from one of the adults. By the time their first winter comes, the pups are ready to join in when the pack hunts.

Leaving Home

A winter of hunting with the pack polishes the young wolves' hunting skill. By spring they are skilled hunters. If their pack is small the young wolves may stay with their parents. But if their pack is too large, they will leave. Some will join with other young wolves and start a new pack of their own. Others will become part of another established pack. In the safety of the pack the wolves may live to be 10 or more years old.

Words to Know

Carnivore   Animal that eats mainly meat.

Den   Animal home.

Guard hairs   Long coarse hairs that make up the outer layer of the wolf's coat.

Litter   The name for the young in one family.

Mate   To come together to produce young.

Pack   A group of as many as 14 wolves, usually related, that live together.

Predator   An animal that hunts other animals for food.

Prey   An animal hunted by another animal for food.

Pup   The name for a young wolf.

Territory   Area that an animal or group of animals lives in and often defends from other animals of the same kind.

Tundra   Flat land in the Arctic where no trees grow.

INDEX

Photo Credits: Stephen J. Krasemann (Valan Photos), pages 4, 8, 12; J.D. Markou (Miller Services), pages 7, 29; Norman Lightfoot (Eco-Art Productions), pages 15, 16, 20; Wayne Lynch (Master File), page 19; Bob Hyland (Valan Photos), pages 23, 43; J.D. Taylor (Miller Services), pages 24, 26; Tim Fitzharris (First Light Associated Photographers), pages 30, 36; Dennis Schmidt (Valan Photos), page 33; Esther Schmidt (Valan Photos), page 34; J.D. Markou (Valan Photos), pages 40, 45.

Printed and Bound in Italy by Lego S[